IT'S TIME TO EAT AN OLIVE

It's Time to Eat an Olive

Walter the Educator

Silent King Books
A WhichHead Entertainment Imprint

Copyright © 2024 by Walter the Educator

All rights reserved. No part of this book may be reproduced in any manner whatsoever without written per- mission except in the case of brief quotations embodied in critical articles and reviews.

First Printing, 2024

Disclaimer

This book is a literary work; the story is not about specific persons, locations, situations, and/or circumstances unless mentioned in a historical context. Any resemblance to real persons, locations, situations, and/or circumstances is coincidental. This book is for entertainment and informational purposes only. The author and publisher offer this information without warranties expressed or implied. No matter the grounds, neither the author nor the publisher will be accountable for any losses, injuries, or other damages caused by the reader's use of this book. The use of this book acknowledges an understanding and acceptance of this disclaimer.

It's Time to Eat an Olive is a collectible early learning book by Walter the Educator suitable for all ages belonging to Walter the Educator's Time to Eat Book Series. Collect more books at WaltertheEducator.com

USE THE EXTRA SPACE TO TAKE NOTES AND DOCUMENT YOUR MEMORIES

OLIVE

It's time to eat an olive,

It's Time to Eat an

Olive

So shiny, small, and round,

They come in black or green, you see,

A treasure to be found!

From groves of trees, they grow so tall,

In sunlight, warm and bright,

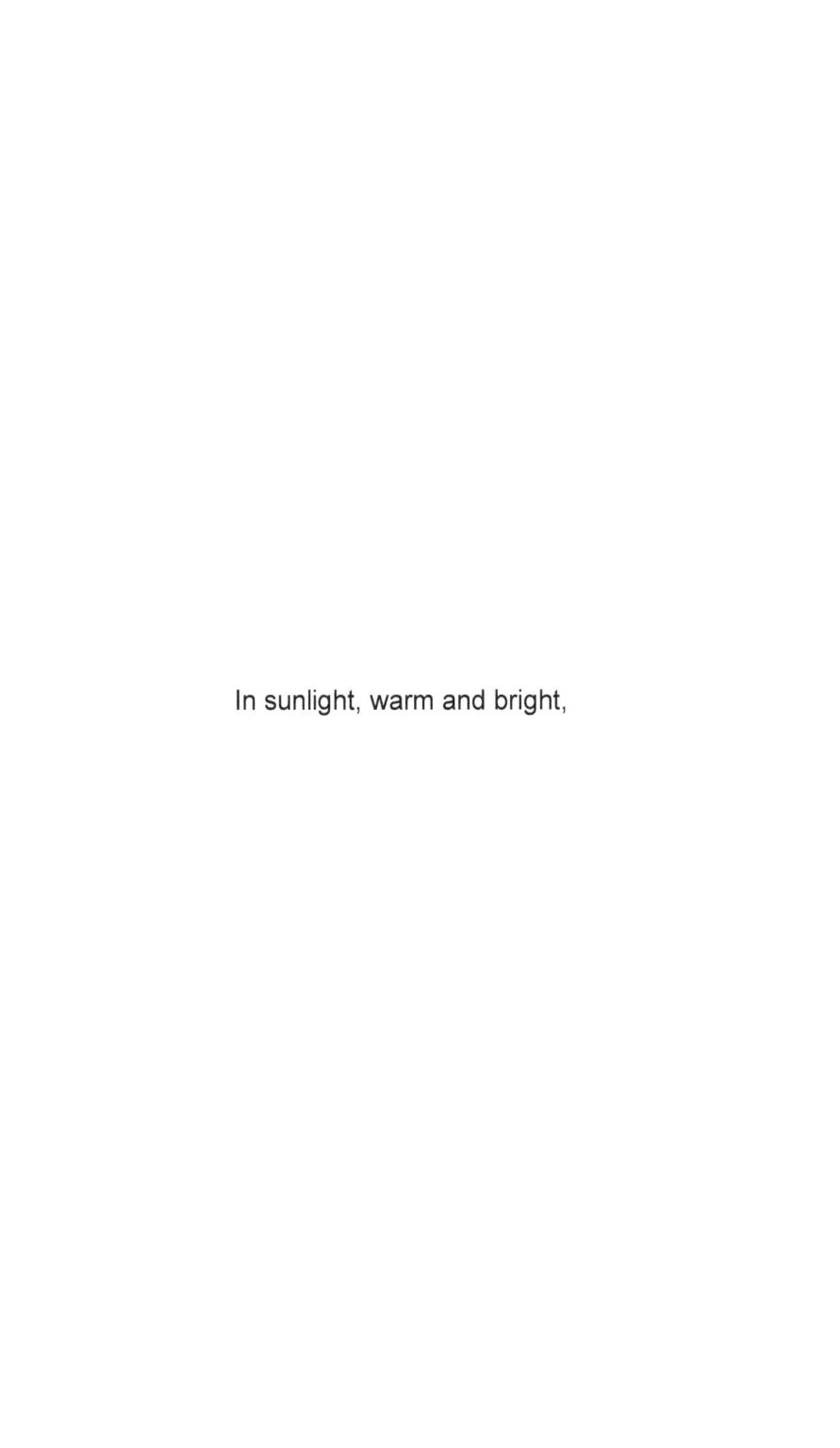

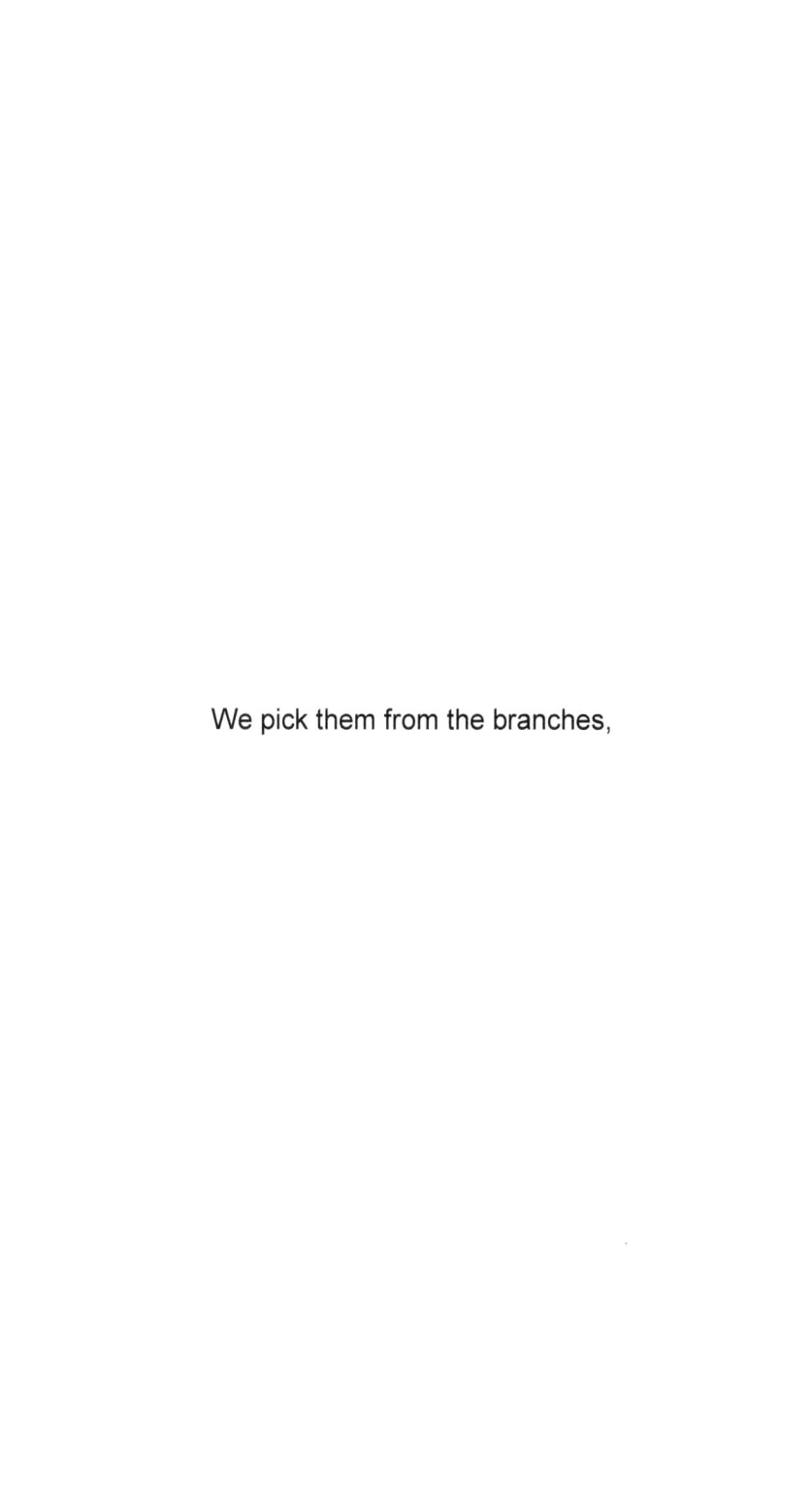

We pick them from the branches,

In the morning or at night.

Some are salty, some are sweet,

Some are soft, some firm to eat,

But each one has a little pit,

That you should not forget to spit!

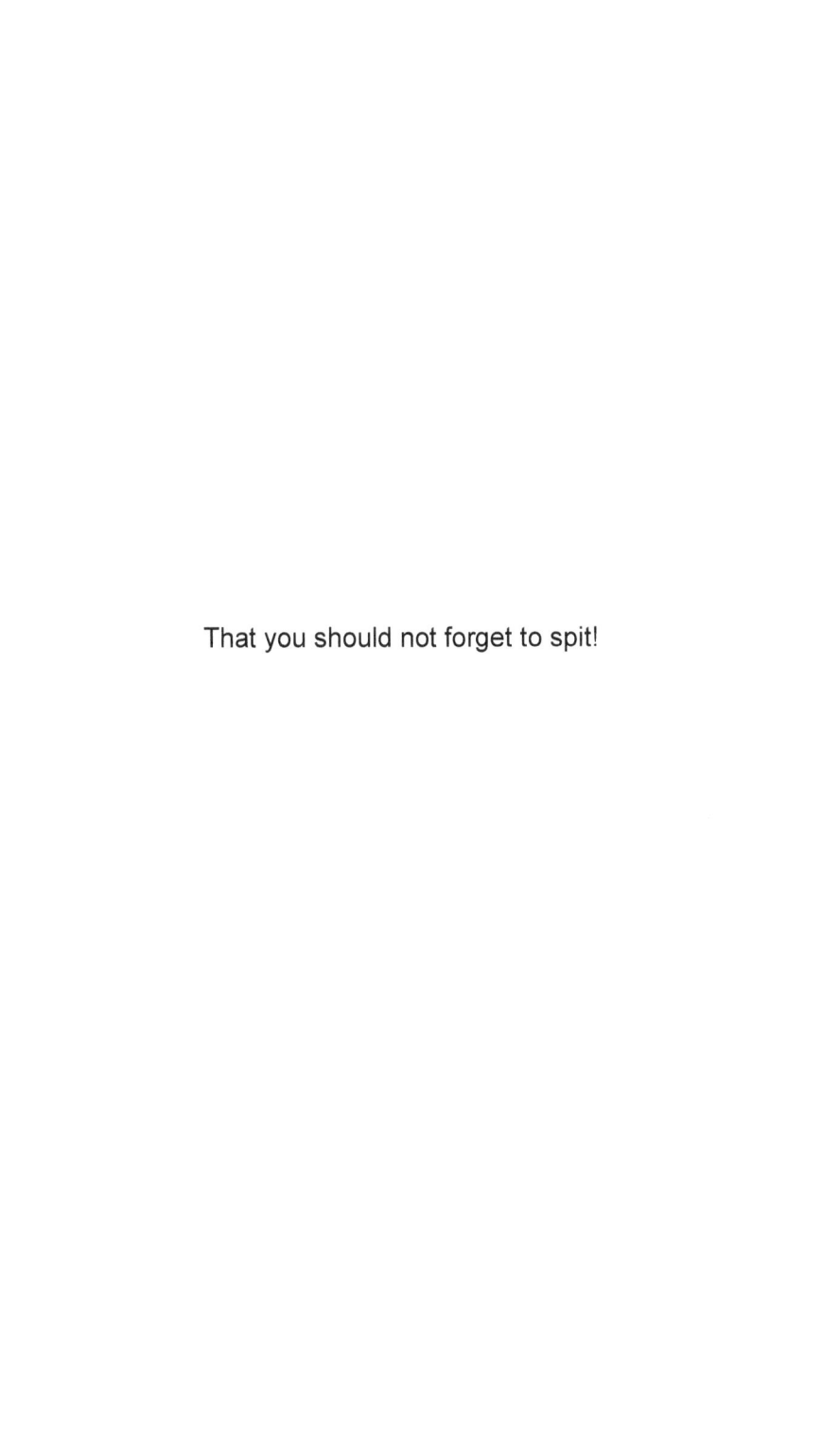

You can eat them on a plate,

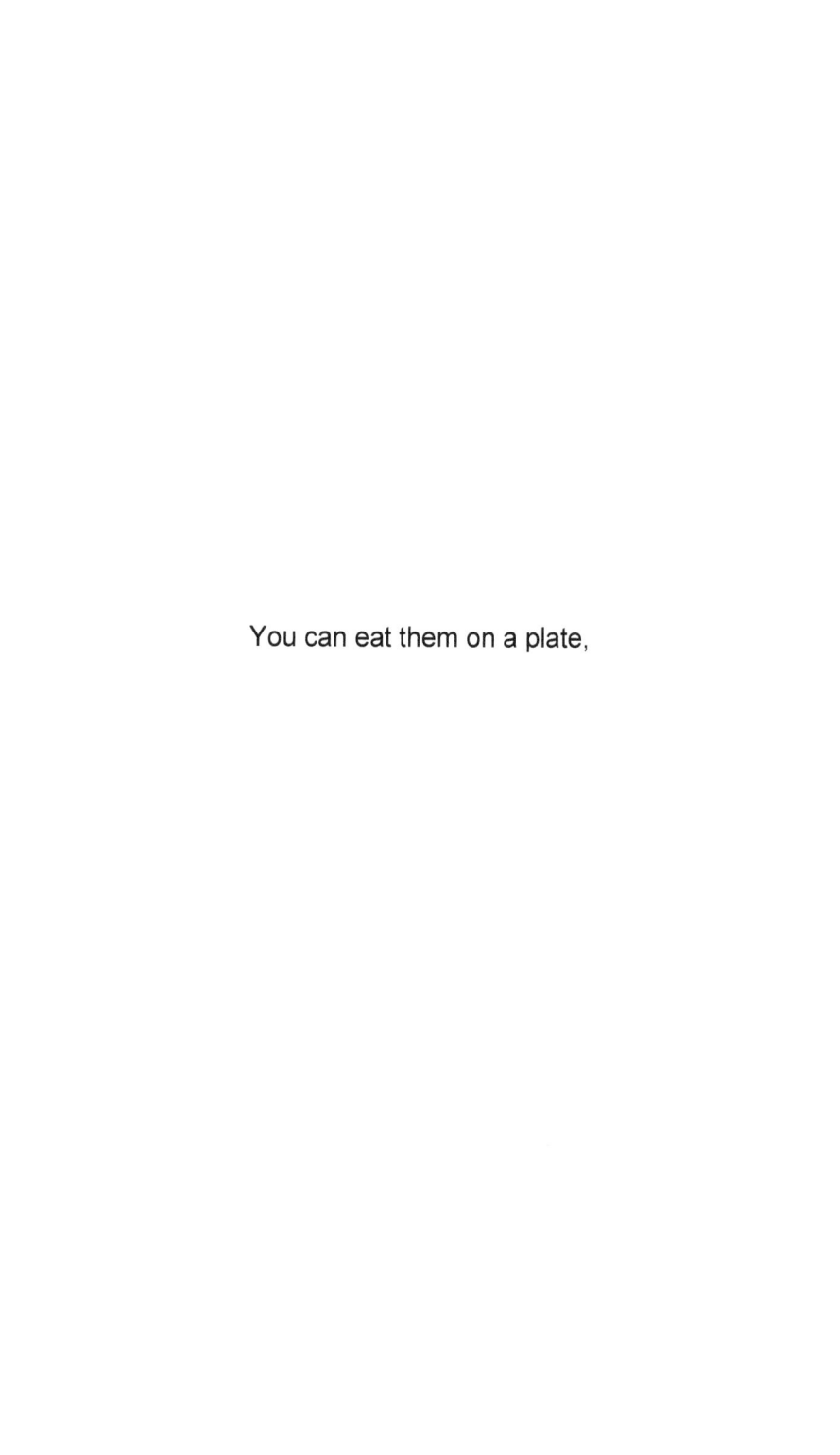

Or pop one in your hand,

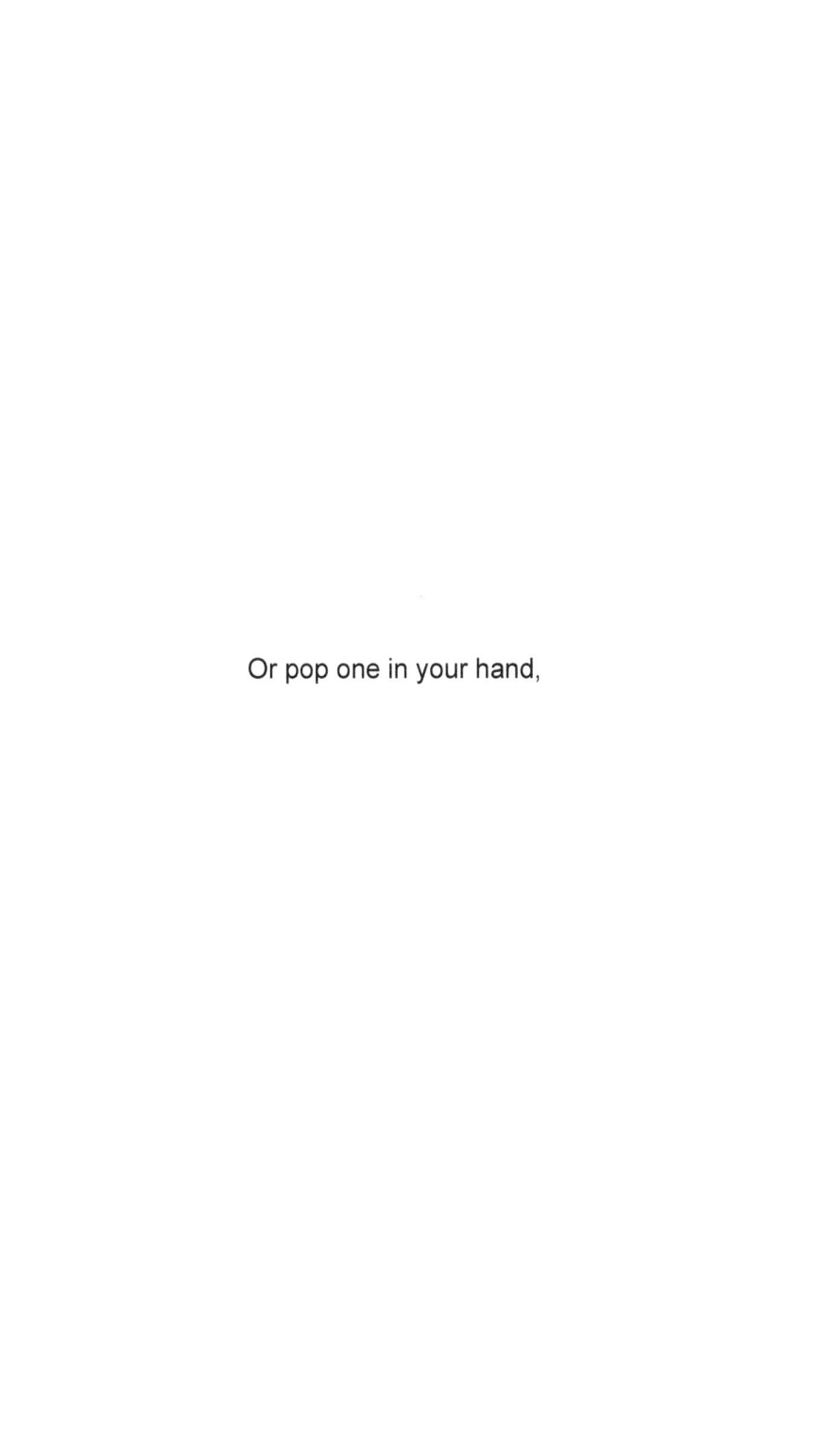

A perfect snack for everyone,

So tasty and so grand!

It's Time to Eat an

Olive

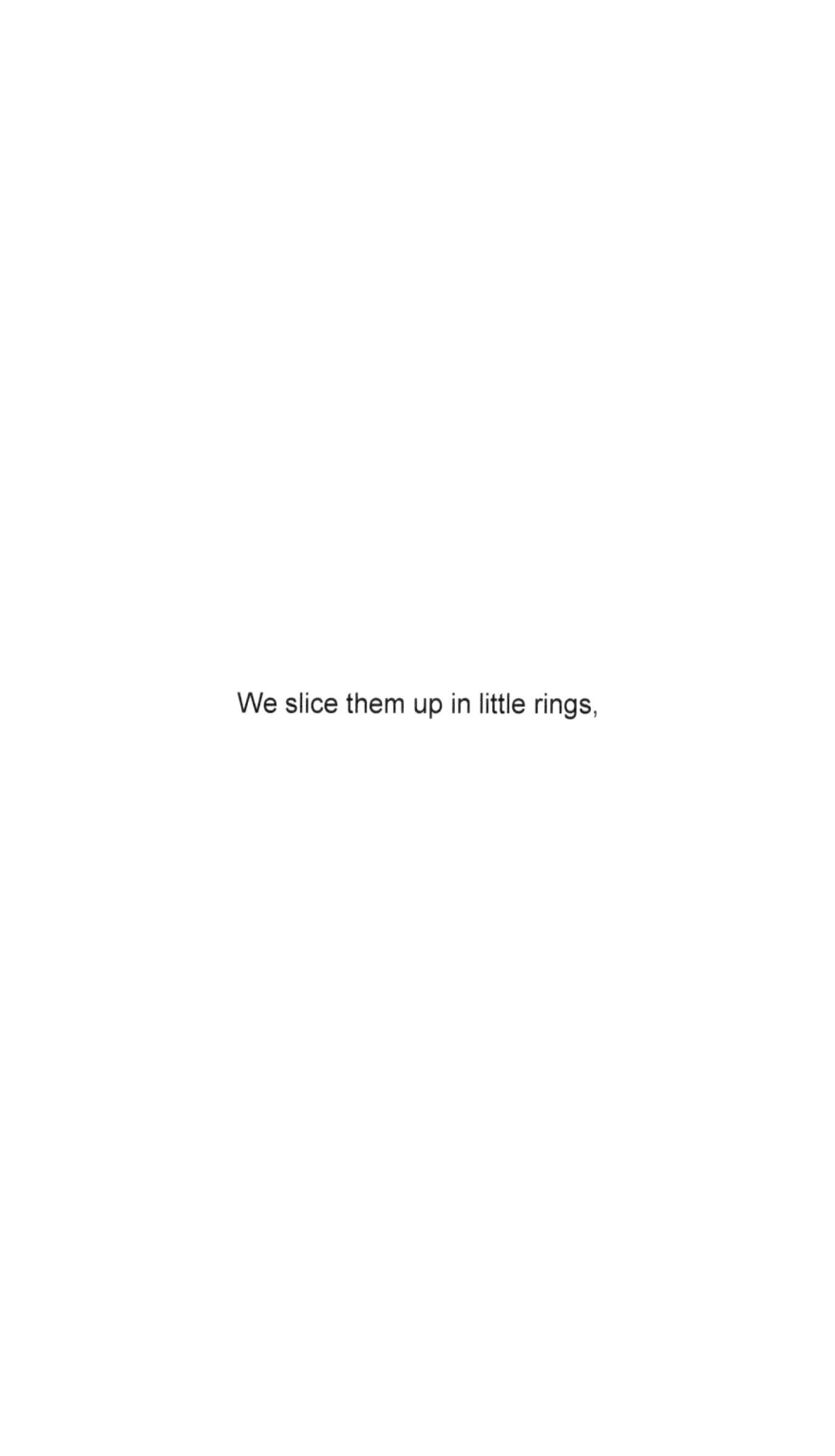
We slice them up in little rings,

And put them on our pizza pies,

Or stuff them full of yummy things,

A tasty little surprise!

In salads they are crunchy friends,

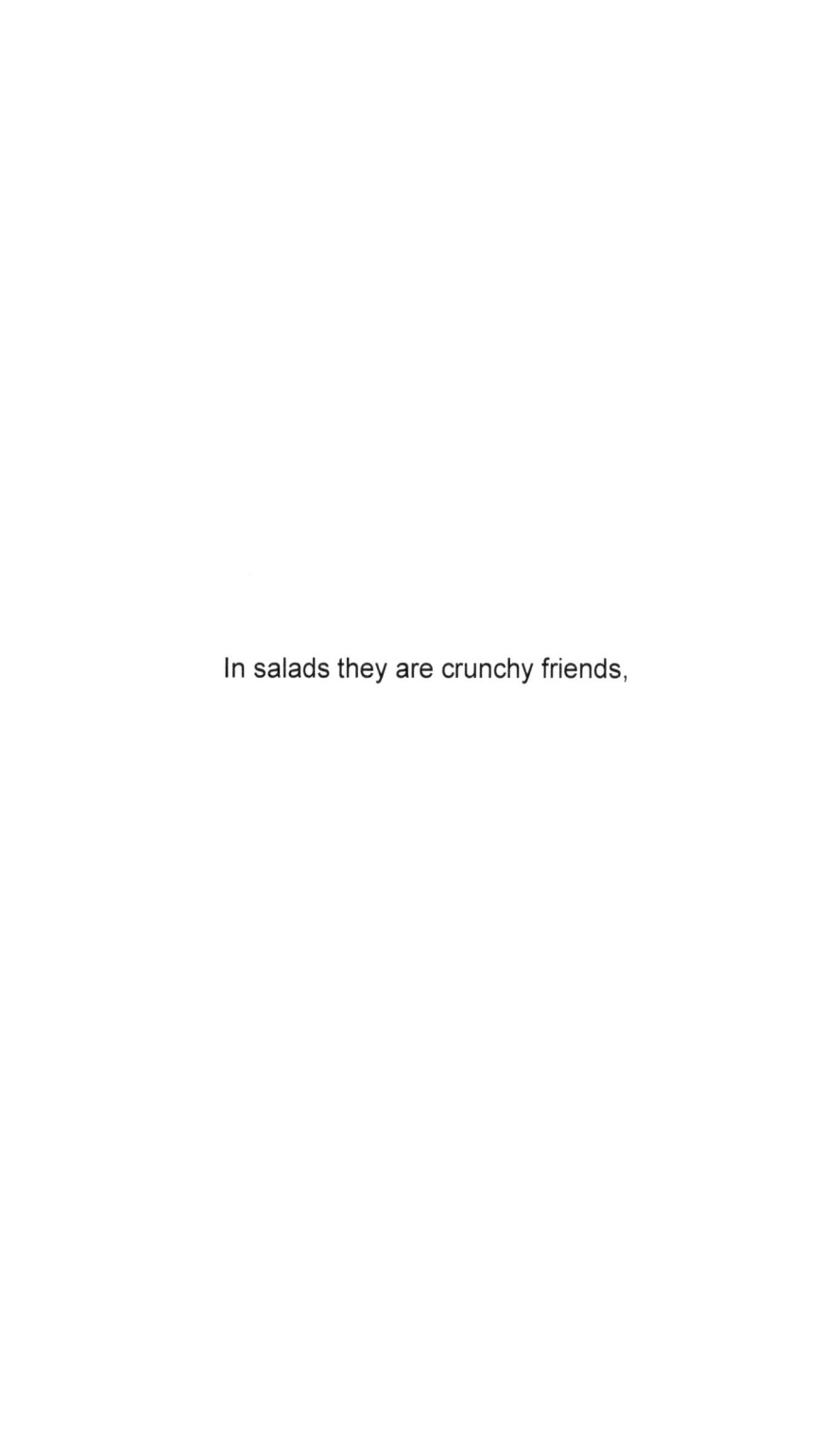

With veggies, cheese, and more,

Olives make each bite so fun,

A treat you can't ignore!

If you try an olive today,

You'll find they're quite a treat,

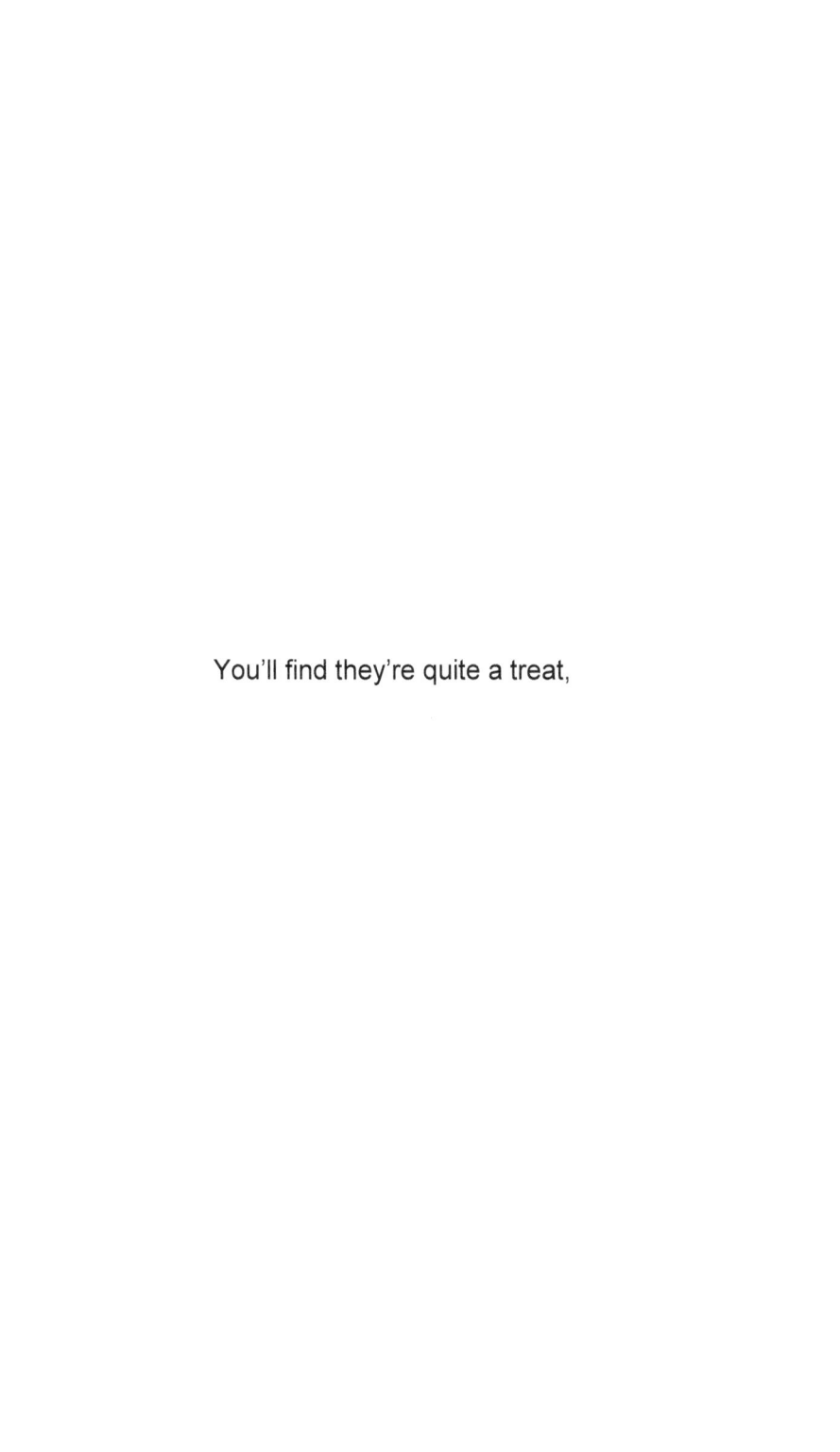

They're packed with flavor, rich and bold,

And oh, so good to eat!

Some are green, and some are black,

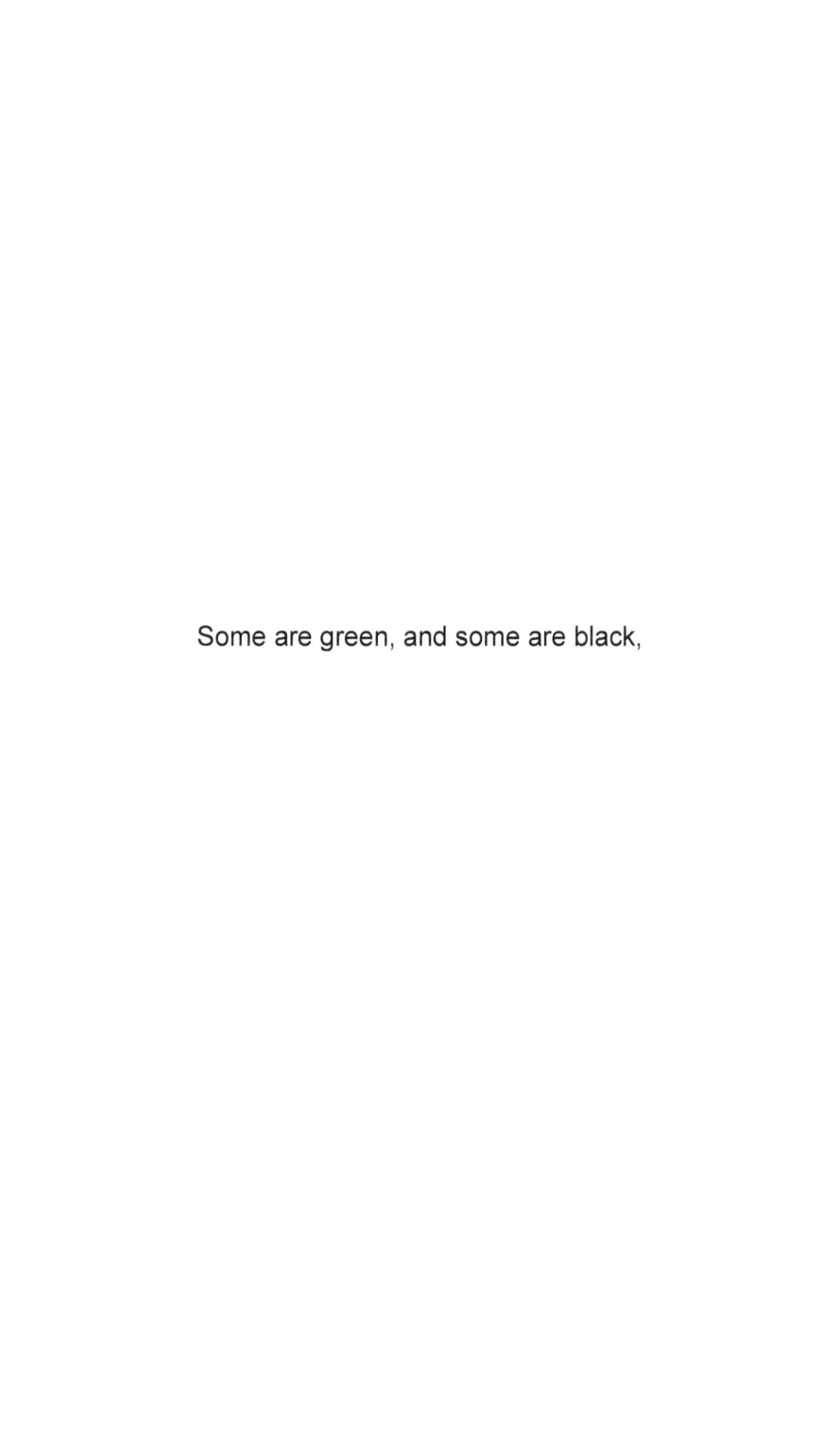

Some are tiny, some are fat,

But every olive's full of cheer,

It's Time to Eat an

Olive

And we're so glad to have them here!

We can mix them in a spread,

Or blend them into dips,

And when you bite into their skin,

You'll love the olive's zips and zings!

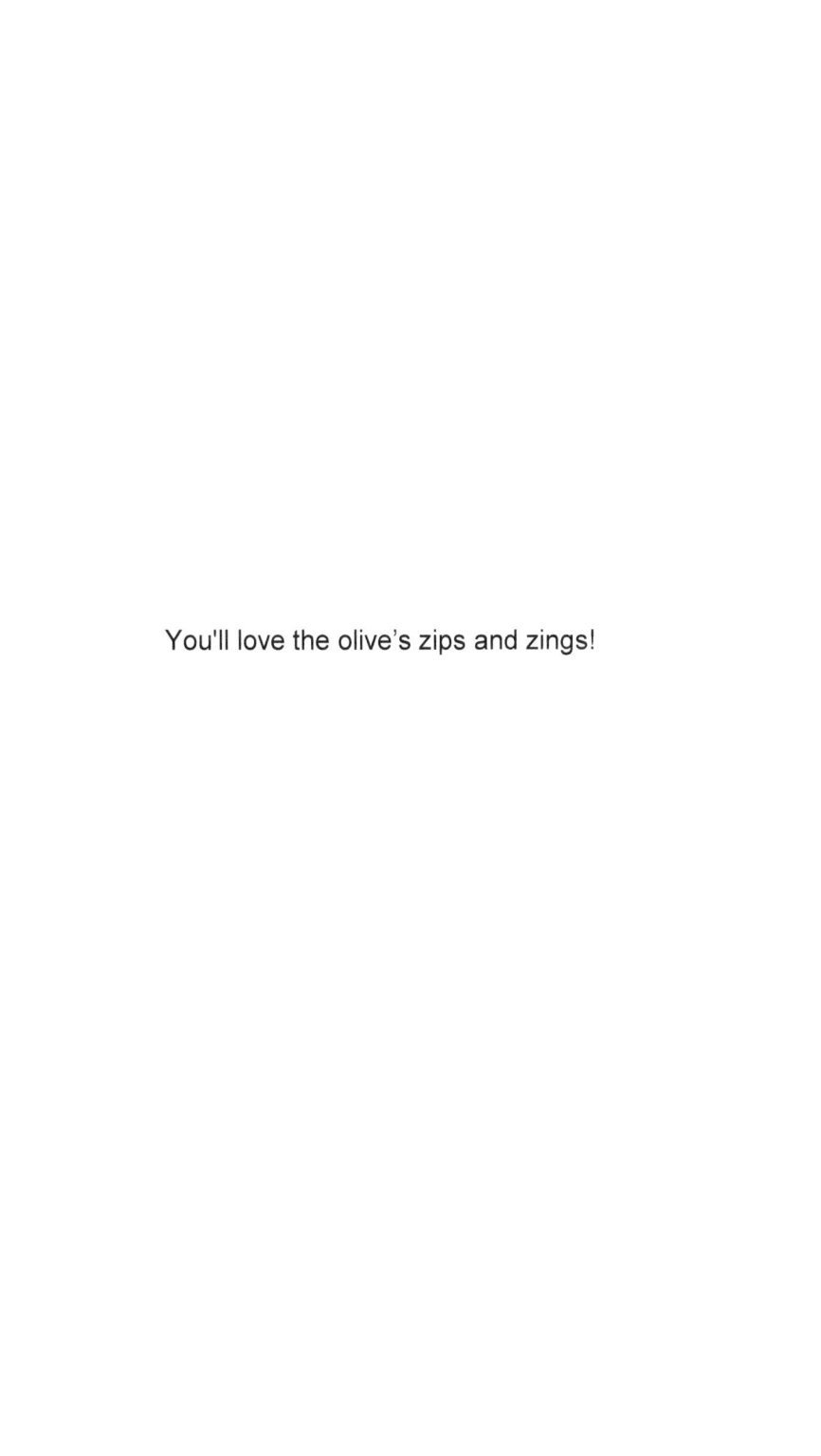

Olives on a sandwich, too,

With bread and cheese piled high,

They add a little extra taste,

A perfect flavor—my oh my!

ABOUT THE CREATOR

Walter the Educator is one of the pseudonyms for Walter Anderson. Formally educated in Chemistry, Business, and Education, he is an educator, an author, a diverse entrepreneur, and he is the son of a disabled war veteran. "Walter the Educator" shares his time between educating and creating. He holds interests and owns several creative projects that entertain, enlighten, enhance, and educate, hoping to inspire and motivate you. Follow, find new works, and stay up to date with Walter the Educator™

at WaltertheEducator.com

Milton Keynes UK
Ingram Content Group UK Ltd.
UKHW032318121024
449481UK00012B/431

9 798330 452514